OVERCOMING FEAR!

UNMASKING THE ENEMIES OF THE CHURCH

DENISE FRANGIPANE

Scripture taken from the New American Standard Bible
© 1960, 1962, 1963, 1968, 1971, 1973, 1975, 1977
by the Lockman Foundation. Used by permission.

Al rights reserved
Printed in the United States of America

ISBN #1#-886296-04-9

Copyright © **1996** Denise Frangipane
Arrow Publications, Inc.
PO Box 10102
Cedar Rapids, IA 52410

CONTENTS

1. Overcoming Fear! 5
2. My Journey 9
3. The Many Faces of Fear 14
4. The Hour of Deliverance 20
5. Discerning the Voice of Defeat 23
6. The Strength of God's Word 29
7. Be Bold and Courageous! 33
8. Use It or Lose It! (by Francis Frangipane) 42

Notes

1.

OVERCOMING FEAR!

Notes

My daughter yells, "Don't look down." I look down and gasp. Again she yells, "Mom, don't look down!" I ignore her pleas and rapidly deplete all the oxygen from our vehicle. We are climbing higher and higher, with no barriers between us and the steep cliffs immediately outside my window.

My husband thinks it's funny, but I am terrified. At every turn, every incline, in my mind we seem to be only an inch from imminent death. Finally we reach our destination: a rental cabin at the top of a mountain in the Great Smokies.

Climbing out of the Jeep, I felt weak and disappointed with myself. Where was my faith? Overwhelmed by my immediate danger, I had given in to fear instead of trusting that God was able to deliver me.

That evening I lay on the bed thinking of the terrible possibilities that could occur on any one of our numerous trips down the mountain. I also thought about avoiding any of these possibilities by just staying by myself and refusing to go anywhere. But our vacation was just beginning. I knew that I must capture my thoughts. I repented of my fears and began laying hold of faith.

Turning my thoughts to prayer, I was reminded of the story of Jesus with His disciples in the boat. It reads, "And behold, there arose a great storm in the sea, so that the boat was covered with the waves; but He Himself was asleep. And they came to Him, and awoke Him, saying, 'Save us, Lord; we are perishing!' And He said to them, 'Why are you timid, you men of little faith?' Then He arose, and rebuked the winds and the sea; and it became perfectly calm" (Matt. 8:24-26).

The disciples were terrified. Even though Jesus was with them, in their minds and to all appearances they were perishing. But they cried out to Jesus to save them and He did. Think about it!

Jesus stood up in the midst of a raging storm and commanded the winds and the sea to be calm, and they obeyed Him. What power and authority! Is there anything too difficult for Him? Now I was ready with renewed faith and trust to face my mountain.

GOD'S GOAL: FEARLESS LIVING

To some degree we are all harassed by fears and anxieties. Whether imagined or real, small or great, these fears rob us of our peace and joy. Yet, these discouraging and intimidating tormentors can be shut out forever.

Fearless, creative living is one of God's gifts to us. Yet, many Christians are shackled and oppressed by fears. Without a doubt, it is time for those fears to be bound and God's children to be set free!

Fear, like a magnifying glass, will exaggerate whatever challenges we gaze upon. Fear always creates the illusion that our problems are bigger than our ability to overcome them. If you have a stronghold of fear in your life, you will often feel frustrated and intimidated by even the smallest tasks. You may have great intentions but you feel inwardly helpless to reach your goals. Although God doesn't want us exploited by fear, there may be times in our lives when we are not only victimized by it, we are paralyzed by it.

Notes

The root of the problem for many of us is in our thought life, which may be used by the devil for evil more often than by God for good. Situations and negative images have been embedded deep in our subconscious minds. Like a file cabinet from hell, these images are projected upon our imaginations any time the devil wants to stop our forward progress.

Consider how many frightening stories and horrifying scenes we have seen in movies and on the news? Our minds have been bombarded over and over again with information about murders, accidents and other misfortunes. These memories sabotage our confidence in God and undermine our view of life. We become more aware of the possibility for something bad to occur than of the potential for good to be worked in all things. Not only does a corrupt imagination provide us with a multitude of harmful expectations, but it is the very substance of the stronghold of fear.

2.

MY JOURNEY

Before I appropriated the gift of Christ's peace, I was always looking for something to distract me from my fears. There were few times when I found myself alone while growing up in a family of eleven. My sense of security came from having people always around me. In fact, I hated being alone, especially in the darkness.

To keep from dealing with my gloomy, fearful thoughts, I would occupy my mind with radio, television or books. When all these distractions were removed, however, I was left with an unending supply of tormenting, disabling thoughts.

The enemy had gained free access to my undisciplined thought life. In fact, even after coming to Christ I was still bound by certain fears. Doctrinally, I knew God was love, but I did not fully comprehend His personal love *for me*. I often carried guilt and condemnation when I stumbled. Not only was I fearful of the world around me, I was also afraid of God and the punishment I thought I deserved.

Even as a parent, when I found myself alone I imagined horrible things that could happen to me or my children. The creaking of the house at night would be exaggerated into footsteps. The sound of the wind outside brought prowlers into my imagination. I lay on my bed (or was it *under* the bed?) paralyzed by fear. I could sense the presence of evil.

Those dark, frightening thoughts became so real they consumed my mind and constantly stirred up my emotions. It seemed that even God Himself had retreated behind the cloud of my oppression.

Because I lacked discernment, I failed to recognize that the devil was the source and manipulator of many of my fears. Even as we can "fix our minds" on the Lord and soon feel His presence, so surrendering to the enemy's manipulation of our minds can bring the manifestation of a spirit of fear.

Of course, the night eventually passed and the things I feared had not occurred. After many years of similar battles, I realized I was missing the abundant life Jesus came to give us; I began to seek the Lord for deliverance.

God's Answer

One night I had a dream. I was standing on a very narrow ledge. I could see nothing; darkness had enveloped me. Balancing on this thin ledge, I was petrified, afraid of falling. All around me I could hear cynical, mocking voices.

In the dream, a light was turned on and I saw that the floor was only a couple of inches below the ledge! *Fear had exaggerated my danger; its darkness had blinded me to reality.* Light broke the illusion and sent the enemy fleeing!

Through this dream the Holy Spirit showed me how Satan was a master illusionist. Any time we open ourselves up to fear, we fall prey to his deceptions and intimidations. Yet, if we submit our hearts to God and stand in faith, we can resist those first fearful thoughts. As we yield to God we can master our reactions to fear and the enemy will soon flee.

Our first place of victory is in believing the truth concerning our relationship with God. Paul tells us that, "having been justified by faith, we have peace with God through our Lord Jesus Christ" (Rom. 5:1). We reject the lie that insists God is our enemy. We come to believe

He is our Helper in the healing of our souls!

John tells us, "this is the victory that has overcome the world—our faith" (1 John 5:4). Faith in what Christ has done and faith in what God has promised empowers us to overcome the world. It is a faith that believes that He will be with us and trusts that He is able to deliver us. This is the victory that overcomes the world.

You see, "God has not given us a spirit of fear" (2 Tim. 1:7 NKJV). Tormenting, debilitating fears are not from the Lord. Paul continues by saying that the nature of the Holy Spirit abiding in us produces a spirit "of power and of love and of a sound mind."

This means that our feelings of helplessness are not from God. We can be assured that, whenever our minds become darkened through self-condemnation, fear or tormenting guilt, we are living outside the realm of God's "love," for God's perfect love "casts out fear" (1 John 4:18).

To win the war against fear, we must know the true God as He is revealed in the Bible. He works to give us lasting peace. He receives joy, not from condemning us but in rescuing us from the devil. Yes, the Lord will bring conviction to our hearts concerning sin, but it is so He can deliver us from sin's power and consequences. In its place, the Lord works to establish healing, forgiveness and peace.

If we walk humbly with the Lord, He promises to lift us up and dwell with us. The effect of God's power and love working in us is a sound mind. Our freedom from fear grows as we grow in God. He came to "destroy the works of the devil" (1 John 3:8) and to set the captives free.

Notes

3.

THE MANY FACES OF FEAR

Besides demonic fears, there are wholesome and natural fears. Fear (or reverence) of the Lord is clean and leads to life. It is also the beginning of both wisdom and knowledge as stated many times in the Scriptures. There are cautionary fears that alert us to danger. Also, there may be times when we are apprehensive and concerned for a situation or for someone.

But *fearfulness, worry* and *anxiety* only lead to doubt and mistrust, which culminate in physical and emotional disorders. We can become so consumed by a problem or situation that, in such a state of mind, we lose sight of who God is and His almighty ability to help us.

Regarding sickness, in some cases people can be so convinced that they may have a particular disease that their mind actually creates symptoms of that disease even though medical tests prove they do not have the illness! Not only can the mind mimic the characteristics of an illness, but many diseases are actually *caused* by stress-related disorders afflicting the mind through fear.

Certainly, there are real problems we must overcome in life, but fear sees only the problem. Faith causes us to look to the Lord in the midst of the problem. Faith inspires us to trust God, enabling us to rest in the Lord's power to cause all things to work for good. Indeed, the Lord tells us in Jeremiah, " 'I know the plans that I have for you,' declares the Lord, 'plans for welfare and not for calamity to give you a future and a hope' " (Jer. 29:11).

Even though fear is an acknowledged enemy of our walk with God, unfortunately we tend to accept pessimistic fears and anxieties as a normal condition of life. David said, "though I walk through the valley of the shadow of death, I will fear no evil, for Thou art with me" (Ps. 23:4). David learned to "fear no evil" and so must we. We must recognize our negative fears as enemies from hell that the Lord calls us to conquer and subdue. If we lose this battle, oppression and bondage await us.

Forms of Fear

Fear manifests in many ways. We may have a fear of the dark, of storms, or of spiders. We may fear for our children's safety and future. Many are afraid of loneliness, aging, sickness and death. Many people fear public speaking. We fear rejection and we fear correction. The list goes on and on.

The Bible declares, "The fear of man brings a snare" (Prov. 29:25). Some of these fears can simply be a wrong response to a legitimate concern, or they can become so established in our thought patterns that they are a dwelling place for demonic activity and oppression.

Fear can be at the root of our hatred toward certain things. When we hate something, frequently it is because we are afraid of it. We may "hate" going to the dentist. The dentist didn't personally do anything to deserve this (usually), but because we fear the discomfort involved in our visit, we come to hate the trip to the dentist. I hated the dark, as I feared someone might attack me.

Fear is the taproot of many of our insecurities. Out of this unstable place many other life-destroying sins emerge. Jealousy is often rooted in fear, as is envy and pride.

When fear becomes a stronghold in our lives, it allows the enemy to hide behind an oppressive pattern of thoughts. These faulty thinking patterns bring us into a life of anxiety and defeat, affliction and oppression. The Word of God tells us that "fear involves torment" (1 John 4:18 NKJV). Such is the life of one tormented by fear.

Fearful thoughts can drain our minds of their creative energy and faith: "What if one of my children dies or has a serious accident?" "What if someone breaks into my house?" "How will I support my family if I contract a disabling disease?" "What if my spouse leaves me for another?"

In a world governed by fears, we graphically imagine evil situations until we become overwhelmed by them. We think we are losing our minds—and in a sense we *are!*

Our problem is that we have failed to discern these thoughts as coming from outside of ourselves. We accept them and think they are our own. Before this whole mind-set begins, we must capture the very first thoughts that do not line up with God's Word.

Even when we are in the midst of real problems, we must never forget we have a real God. He is with us always. Because the Redeemer is in our lives, we can trust that even what originates with the devil himself, God will use for good. In Genesis 50:20, Joseph says of his brothers, "you meant evil against me, but God meant it for good."

Promises That Build Our Faith

The Word tells us that God has given His angels charge concerning us, to minister and protect. "The angel of the Lord encamps around those who fear Him, and rescues them" (Ps. 34:7).

Instead of yielding to fear when alone, I began to use my imagination. I would picture a guarding angel encamped on the lawn of my home. His sword was always ready at his side and his senses alert for any intruders. No roasting marshmallows or playing solitaire at this camp. How secure I felt knowing that he was there for my protection.

"Those who trust in the Lord are as Mount Zion, which cannot be moved, but abides forever. As the mountains surround Jerusalem, so the Lord surrounds His people from this time forth and forever" (Ps. 125:1-2). Again I would imagine the Lord and His angels surrounding my home as the mountains surround Jerusalem.

Before David was king, Saul hunted him and sought to kill him. David hid in the caves with his mighty men. Though he feared for his life, he was not a fearful, cowering wimp but a strong and courageous warrior. David's strength came in his worship. He sang, "Thou art my hiding place; Thou dost preserve me from trouble; Thou dost surround me with songs of deliverance" (Ps. 32:7). David trusted in the Lord and he was not afraid.

Notes

4.
THE HOUR OF DELIVERANCE

I was tormented by both fear and anxiety for many years before my victory. As a result, I suffered from ulcerated colitis, spastic colon and other illnesses. I could not assimilate food properly and my weight ranged between 89 and 92 pounds. I had chronic fatigue and countless headaches. I became so thin that my husband would often lovingly introduce me not as his "better half," but his "better *third.*"

Finally, in desperation I told the Lord I could not live in this condition any longer. I was determined to change even if I were to die in the process. I began to wholeheartedly seek God with fasting and prayer. For days I did not eat and could barely sleep. I was so sick from the acid burning in my colon, inflamed joints and severe headaches, I thought I was dying. In my frame of mind, I actually would have welcomed the release. Yet in spite of my constant pain, I had the most wonderful, intimate time of communion with the Lord.

He revealed to me that the source of my physical problems came from anxiety and fear. They were not "normal conditions of life"; they were sins of mistrust and unbelief that were keeping me from living in the ppreresence of God. They carried consequences that often isolated me from the will of God. As such, these were unacceptable and I needed to repent of them.

On the fourth night of fasting, I remained kneeling as I sought God into the early morning. My mind was being harassed with certain thoughts that had plagued me for years. As I cried to God for help, a spirit of fear actually appeared at my side. *But the Lord told me this was my hour of deliverance!* I was about to be delivered from the spirit that had been warring against me all my life.

As I repented for allowing fear and anxiety to exist in my life, immediately a great peace entered my soul. My mind was finally at rest. The following day I experienced complete healing and went

Notes

Notes

for the next few months eating just about everything in sight with no symptoms of sickness. Of course, I wouldn't suggest that for everyone.

If God had just healed my symptoms, I would have certainly become sick again. God wanted me to deal with the cause of my disease. Desperation led me to repentance; repentance broke my emotional union with the spirit of fear, enabling God to bring healing to my body.

I can truthfully agree with the psalmist who wrote, "I considered my ways, and turned my feet to Thy testimonies" (Ps. 119:59) and, "Before I was afflicted I went astray, but now I obey Thy word" (v. 67).

5.

Notes

DISCERNING THE VOICE OF DEFEAT

Paul says, "For this reason God will send upon them a deluding influence so that they might believe what is false, in order that they all may be judged who did not believe the truth, but took pleasure in wickedness" (2 Thess. 2:11-12). Our lives are easily drawn into confusion and deluding influences when we harbor unbelief. If we don't "believe the truth," it is impossible to be set free. Instead, we continually "believe what is false," suffering serious consequences.

Now, there is a difference between accumulating facts and knowing the truth about ourselves. *Facts* are based on

Notes

things that really happened in our lives. *Truth* unlocks all the potential God has placed in us.

God calls us a new creation, created in His likeness. This is the *truth* about us. We can "do all things through Christ who strengthens (us)" (Phil. 4:13). If we believe only the facts as the world defines them, we are actually believing lies! Instead, we need to believe the promises of God for our lives.

Voices of defeat and discouragement often emerge from our past. These voices are fed by our past failures and are reinforced by the destructive words of those we respected. "You're no good," an angry father uttered. You believed it and became "no good." "You'll never amount to anything," said a frustrated teacher. From that moment on, an invisible barrier stood between you and any hope that you could "amount to anything."

Even now, doubt and failure fill our opinions of ourselves. Instead of being filled with faith, we become filled with fear regarding our future. We wallow in defeat, remembering our past failures. But Jesus said *His* truth will set us free. Knowing the truth and believing it is the beginning of that freedom.

God has saved us so He might reveal His glory in us. "It was for this [God] called you through our gospel, that you may gain the glory of our Lord Jesus Christ" (2 Thess. 2:14). Even though we are called to gain the glory of Christ, *access* to God's provision is impossible if we do not *believe* the truth of God's Word.

SHATTERING THE TEETH OF OUR ENEMY

David prayed, "O Lord, how my adversaries have increased! Many are rising up against me. Many are *saying* of my soul, 'There is no deliverance for him in God' " (Ps. 3:1-2).

David was surrounded by enemies within and without. He cried out, "Arise, O Lord; save me, O my God! For thou has smitten all my enemies on the cheek; Thou hast shattered the teeth of the wicked" (vv. 7-8). God broke the *jaws* of David's enemies. He shut their mouths. He stopped the lying, accusing, condemning voices that were a source of conflict for David. We, too, must cease listening to the voices of our enemies!

A sure way to see God shut the mouths of your adversaries is through praise and worship. When Jehoshaphat heard he was surrounded by a great multitude of foes, he was afraid. He cried out to the Lord in his distress and the Lord heard him. He was told, "do not fear or be dismayed because of this great multitude, for the battle is not yours but God's" (2 Chron. 20:15).

Jehoshaphat appointed those who praised the Lord. They put on holy attire and went before Israel's army singing and giving thanks to the Lord. As

> **Notes**

they did, God set up ambushes and routed the enemy. God inhabits our praises. His presence goes before us and He destroys our enemies.

Not only will God cause the voices of our enemies to cease, but He will also put a bridle on our mouths as well! Our confession of doubt and unbelief is lethal to our walk with God. Our tongues set the course for our lives, whether for a life of victory or defeat.

"I sought the Lord, and He answered me, and delivered me from all my fears. They looked to Him and were radiant, and their faces shall never be ashamed" (Ps. 34:4–5).

When we look to the Lord and put our trust in Him we find peace and courage; we radiate confidence. When we look at our circumstances and lose heart, our countenance falls; we give in to defeat.

What is it that causes us to want to hide our face in shame? Most of the time it is sin but often it is our failures. We are afraid to fail because we remember the humiliation or rejection we suffered when we stepped out and didn't immediately succeed.

When I first began to teach, my mind would sometimes go blank and I'd forget the point I was trying to make. I would look frantically to my notes for help, only to be rewarded with a mass of blurry letters. Then, gazing up nervously at the many faces in front of me, I would notice several yawning people. After this happened a few times, I decided I could not stand the humiliation. I pledged I would never teach again. A stronghold of fear was created and held me captive for almost fifteen years.

Every time I was asked to teach, *fear* became my unseen foe, swooping over my heart. Inwardly, my mind would scream, *No, I can't! No, I won't!* Fear paralyzed me and prevented me from fulfilling God's call on my life. Knowing I was disobeying the Lord, I would end up in condemnation. Eventually, I put up a big wall between God and myself.

One day I had just finished a one-sided "conversation" with my husband. I was wallowing in self-pity, feeling pathetic and looking for sympathy. Not receiving any from him, I threw myself on the bed and just cried to the Lord: "Lord, I'm so tired of this struggle. Help me!" The Holy Spirit led me to Isaiah 43:18-19: "Do not call to mind the former things, or ponder things of the past. Behold, I will do something new, now it will spring forth; will you not be aware of it?"

It was as though the Lord was telling me, *Look, I'm not remembering the things of the past, why should you? Stop dwelling on your failures because I am about to do a new thing!* Then He led me to Isaiah 54:4. He told me, "Fear not, for you will not be put to shame; neither feel humiliated, for you will not be disgraced; but you will forget the shame of your youth, and the reproach of your widowhood you will remember no more" (Isa. 54:4).

Now I began to weep tears of joy. God through His Word was giving me a promise. Standing on this promise, I had confidence to cast off fear and with joy walk in obedience to the Lord. I knew I could aim toward excellence and have success.

The promise of the Lord to each of us resounds with His love. He says, "In righteousness you will be established; you will be far from oppression, for you will not fear" (Isa. 54:20). This is the heart of God! He comes to defeat and silence the voices of our enemies.

6.

THE STRENGTH OF GOD'S WORD

Moses had asked the Lord to tell him His divine name. In reply, the Lord answered, "And God said to Moses, 'I AM WHO I AM'; and He said, 'Thus you shall say to the sons of Israel, I AM has sent me to you' " (Ex. 3:14).

When the Lord identified Himself as the great "I AM," He was saying to everyone who wants to know Him, *I am who I say I am and will be to you all that I AM.* His name is Jehovah Jireh, our provider; Jehovah Ra-ah, our Shepherd; Jehovah Shalom, the Lord our Peace; Jehovah Shammah, an ever-present help; Jehovah Rapha, our Healer. You can be sure that

God is who He says He is and will be to us all that we believe Him to be. He is faithful. He stands behind His Word.

It is upon this faithfulness of the Lord's covenant nature that our lives are established. A child who is confident in the love of his parents will not fear punishment when he has disobeyed but will know that he will be justly disciplined. Whereas a child who has been disciplined out of frustration and anger will anxiously fear the punishment coming to him. God, our Father, disciplines us out of love, for our own good. He does not want us to remain as children but to grow up in all aspects of Christ.

Early in our ministry, my husband would occasionally leave overnight to teach Bible studies in Canada. I would be left alone with our two young children. At that time, I did not know how to discern those fearful, tormenting thoughts as demonic influences. One evening I was overcome by terror. I sat curled up on the couch crying and unable to move. My three-year-old daughter, Joy, was awakened by the Lord. She came to me, eyes heavy with sleep, and said, "Mommy, Jesus told me to tell you, 'Do not fear, I am with you. I will never leave you nor forsake you.'" Jesus loved me enough to personally speak to my need.

I picked up my Bible and opened randomly to Isaiah 43:1-3. The Lord's Word read, "Do not fear, for I have redeemed you; I have called you by name; you are Mine! When you pass through the waters, I will be with you; and through the rivers, they will not overflow you. When you walk through the fire, you will not be scorched, nor will the flame burn you. For I am the Lord your God, the Holy One of Israel, your Savior."

I could feel my heart being liberated by the power of the Word. In Isaiah 41:10, the Lord again spoke to my heart: "Do not fear, for I am with you; Do not anxiously look about you, for I am your God. I will strengthen you, surely I will help you, surely I will uphold you with My righteous right hand."

He has made it possible for us to be partakers of His divine nature. He has made us overcomers through His Spirit that indwells us. The same Spirit that raised Jesus Christ from the dead lives in us, giving life to our mortal bodies. If we could truly grasp this revelation, we would no longer be oppressed by sin and sickness, doubt and fear. We would rise up and possess the glorious, powerful overcoming nature of Christ.

God has declared that His goal for us is nothing less than full transformation into His nature. He assures us that, "As He is, so also are we in this world" (1 John 4:17). This spiritual stature makes us more than typical Christians. Jesus is the living, trium-

Notes

phant, exalted Son of God who reigns in glory and power in us! He is a mighty conqueror, victorious over all the powers of darkness in us! He is our glorious High Priest unto God, interceding *for us.*

You see, there is power in the Word, but only as it dwells in us. It is not enough to hear a good message on Sunday mornings. It is not enough to regularly read Christian books or view Christian television: we must know God's Word to experience God's power.

The Word of God is so powerful. Each time we come across a promise that stirs our hearts, we should record it in a notebook. His Word contains love letters from the Bridegroom, marching orders from the Captain of the Hosts, food from heaven, and healing for illness. Weekly, we should review the promises we have written, study them, pray over them, memorize them, and make them our own. We will bring the great I AM nature of God into every one of our circumstances!

7.

BE BOLD AND COURAGEOUS!

TRUE FAITH TAKES COURAGE!

We don't all live in the inner cities, surrounded by poverty, drugs and gang activities. Some of us have never experienced the anguish that parents of children who have been murdered or kidnaped or lost to the devil have. We do not live in a country where Christians are being blatantly persecuted for their faith. Yet fear is the stronghold that keeps God's people bound and enslaved.

We must face the reality that Jesus came to save us, to heal us, and to change

Notes

us into His likeness, but He did not say that we wouldn't have to suffer. However, He won't allow us to suffer more than we are able to handle. And He promised to be with us and to give us strength to endure.

As we continue to come closer to the end times, the potential to become overwhelmed by the conditions in the world will cause men's hearts to faint with fear. Yet, it is in this very context that Jesus calls us to lift up our heads, for our redemption is drawing near. Our hope is in Jesus. His grace is sufficient.

Remember what the Lord promised Joshua? He told His servant, "Just as I have been with Moses, I will be with you; I will not fail you or forsake you. Be strong and courageous" (Josh. 1:5-6).

Again in verses 7-9, He said, "Only be strong and very courageous; be careful to do according to all the law which Moses My servant commanded you; do not turn from it to the right or to the left, so that you may have success wherever you go. This book of the law shall not depart from your mouth, but you shall meditate on it day and night, so that you may be careful to do according to all that is written in it; for then you will make your way prosperous, and then you will have success. Have I not commanded you? Be strong and courageous! Do not tremble or be dismayed, for the Lord your God is with you wherever you go."

It is God's desire that we be bold and courageous, not fearful and unbelieving, faltering in our faith, cowering and complaining. Real faith takes courage! Joshua and Caleb were men of faith. They were of a different spirit than the rest of the Israelites.

All of the generation over twenty years of age that made the Exodus out of Egypt died in the wilderness, except for Joshua and Caleb. In order for them to have success over their enemies and walk in the favor of the Lord, they needed to obey the Lord and daily delight in God's Word.

"How blessed is the man who does not walk in the counsel of the wicked, nor stand in the path of sinners, nor sit in the seat of scoffers! But his delight is in the law of the Lord, and in His law he meditates day and night.... And in whatever he does, he prospers" (Ps.1:1-3).

In Joshua, chapter six, the Israelites were instructed by God to keep themselves from the things under the ban, lest they covet them and make Israel accursed. Achan disobeyed the ban and hid some of the spoil from Jericho in his tent. His disobedience caused Israel to lose their next battle against Ai. After Israel was defeated, Joshua fell on his face in repentance. The Lord said to him,

Notes

"Rise up! Why is it that you have fallen on your face? Israel has sinned, and they have also transgressed My covenant which I commanded them. And they have even taken some of the things under the ban (things devoted to destruction) and have both stolen and deceived. Moreover they have also put them among their own things.

"Therefore the sons of Israel cannot stand before their enemies; they turn their backs before their enemies, for they have become accursed (made vulnerable). I will not be with you anymore unless you destroy the things under the ban from your midst.

"Rise up! Consecrate the people and say, 'Consecrate yourselves for tomorrow, for thus the Lord, the God of Israel, has said, "There are things under the ban in your midst, O Israel. You cannot stand before your enemies until you have removed the things under the ban from your midst" ' " (Josh. 7:10-13).

The Israelites were told not to take the gold or the silver for themselves, for these were devoted to the Lord. Their greed, however, caused them to both steal and deceive. This act of disobedience brought destruction and a curse upon Israel.

When the Israelites were in right standing with God they were invincible, because God was with them. However, their disobedience made them vulnerable and unable to face their enemies; they turned their backs and fled instead.

There are areas in our lives as well that are "devoted to destruction," that is, they make us vulnerable to the enemy if we allow them among our possessions. Lust, ambition, pride, anger, unbelief, etc., will weaken our faith, hinder our walk, and cause us to lose courage. Sin will separate us from that intimate fellowship with God. By consecrating ourselves to God we gain confidence to enter God's presence, and from that place we find courage to face and defeat our enemies.

"Since therefore, brethren, we have confidence to enter the holy place by the blood of Jesus, by a new and living way which He inaugurated for us through the veil, that is, His flesh, and since we have a great priest over the house of God, let us draw near with a sincere heart in full assurance of faith, having our hearts sprinkled clean from an evil conscience and our bodies washed with pure water" (Heb. 10:19-22).

THERE IS NO FEAR IN LOVE

As we grow in our relationship with Jesus, "we have come to know and have believed the love which God has for us" (1 John 4:16). John continues, "God is love, and the one who abides in love abides in God, and God abides in him. By this, love is perfected with us, that we may have confidence in the day of judgment; because as He is, so also are we in this world" (vv. 16–17). What a tremendous promise! In this world we can actually be as Christ is in heaven.

John continues, "There is no fear in love; but perfect love casts out fear, because fear involves punishment, and the one who fears is not perfected in love" (1 John 4:18).

God promises us, "I have given you authority . . . over all the power of the enemy, and nothing shall injure you" (Luke 10:19). By the blood of Jesus and the Word of God we have authority over every enemy of our soul. Just as Simon prophesied, that we, "being delivered from the hand of our enemies, might serve [God] without fear" (Luke 1:74).

Would you pray with me? *Lord, I repent of the sin of fear. I want only a righteous and holy fear of You that overcomes the fear of everything else. I thank You, Lord Jesus, for Your power over my enemies and Your steadfast love over my life. By the power of Your love, I renounce the stronghold of fear; I enter the stronghold of Your presence. In Jesus' Name, Amen.*

SEVEN STEPS TO FREEDOM

It is important that we prepare ourselves now for a fearless life! If we don't, fear will take us under and swallow us up. We each must rise against it with the sword of the Lord and the shield of faith. Therefore, study these principles along with other Scriptures the Lord has given you. By the power of the Word of God you will be able to overcome each battle against fear.

1. Remember, God loves you!

"And we know that God causes all things to work together for good to those who love God, to those who are called according to His purpose" (Rom. 8:28).

2. Resist the enemy!

Rebuke every fearful thought. "Submit therefore to God. Resist the devil and he will flee from you. Draw near to God and He will draw near to you" (James 4:7-8).

3. Consecrate yourself!

Repent of the specific sins in your life that may be related to this battle. Appropriate the cleansing blood of Jesus so that you will have confidence to stand (see Heb. 10:19-22).

4. Pray!

" 'Have faith in God. Truly I say to you, whoever says to this mountain, "Be taken up and cast into the sea," and does not doubt in his heart, but believes that what he says is going to happen, it shall be granted him. Therefore I say to you, all things for which you pray and ask, believe that you have received them, and they shall be granted you' " (Mark 11:22-24).

5. Fight!

Don't give up. Don't give in. Fight the fight of faith. Use the Word of God to stand against the enemy. "Take up the full armor of God, that you may be able to resist in the evil day, and having done everything, to stand firm" (Eph. 6:13).

6. Worship!

Job, in the midst of devastating trials and tribulations, bowed down and worshiped God. Likewise, let us worship God and remember who He is: Jehovah our Provider, our Healer, our Comforter and our Friend. He is almighty and powerful and there is nothing too difficult for Him.

7. Trust!

How can we trust someone we don't know? We must daily seek to know Him. Through His words we build our trust in Him and gain intimate fellowship with Him.

"Be anxious for nothing, but in everything by prayer and supplication with thanksgiving let your requests be made known to God. And the peace of God, which surpasses all comprehension, shall guard your hearts and your minds in Christ Jesus" (Phil. 4:6–7).

Notes

8.

USE IT OR LOSE IT!

A Message from Francis Frangipane

Each of us has received a special gift, or perhaps several gifts, from God that He wants us to use. Yet, one of the reasons many Christians do not use or develop their spiritual gifts is because of fear. Fear, as Denise stated earlier, will paralyze our creativity and smother our abilities. If we are afraid to fail, which often occurs on the road to success, we become afraid to try new things or creative approaches. It is my experience that the biggest mistake we can make is to be afraid to make mistakes!

Yet, the Scriptures are plain: God expects us to use the talents and resources that

He gives us. With this in mind, Jesus used a parable to teach His disciples the importance of using what He gives us. He told of a nobleman who left to receive a kingdom for himself. While he was gone, he gave to his servants some money with which to do business. When he returned he called his slaves to himself "in order that he might know what business they had done" (Luke 19:15).

"The first appeared, saying, 'Master, your mina has made ten minas more' " (v. 16). The master congratulated his slave because of his faithfulness and put him in authority over ten cities. "And the second came, saying, 'Your mina, master, has made five minas' " (v. 18). The second he also commended and put over five cities.

However, a third appeared before him. This slave had done nothing with his gift. The slave said, "Master, behold your mina, which I kept put away in a handkerchief; for I was afraid of you, because you are an exacting man; you take up what you did not lay down, and reap what you did not sow" (Luke 19:20-21).

The master used this slave's own view of life to judge his behavior, saying, " 'By your own words I will judge you, you worthless slave. Did you know that I am an exacting man, taking up what I did not lay down, and reaping what I did not sow? Then why did you not put the money in the bank, and having come, I would have collected it with interest?' And he said to the bystanders, 'Take the mina away from him, and give it to the one who has the ten minas.' " (vv. 22-24).

Notes

Each of the individuals in the parable was given the resources necessary with which to work. Each used what the master gave him except the one who was afraid. He buried the resource and returned it unused to his master. Interestingly, the one who had just one mina— who actually had the least asked of him—was the most reluctant to get involved. His answer betrayed several unrighteous qualities of heart.

First he said, "I was afraid of you." Note that fear is not a valid excuse for disobeying the Lord. Whether we are afraid or not, God still requires we do what He tells us. A deeper look into this parable reveals *why* this individual was afraid: "because you are an exacting man."

The reason this servant was fearful was because he had a false image of God. God is not exacting. He is not hard and judgmental. In fact, the other servants returned to their master with joy and surprise, saying, "Master, your mina has made ten minas more." They credited the master's mina as being the source of their increase. They simply *used* it and *it* "made ten minas more!"

This is the wonderful mystery about the gifts of God: The more we use them, the more they increase on their own. *God's gifts have the power to multiply and prosper on their own!* The Lord is wonderful, generous and helpful, not exacting!

Matthew's version of this parable adds an insight to Jesus' evaluation of this one-mina-servant and his excuse. He pierces into the *real* motives of this slave's heart and calls him a **"wicked, lazy slave"** (Matt. 25:26).

Again we are reminded that fear is not a valid justification for disobedience. In reality, it could be a smokescreen for rebellion and laziness.

The wonderful thing, however, is that once we set our hearts to use what God has given us, and do so for His glory, a wonderful grace enters our lives. Having *just* a religion evaporates as God's Spirit gently expands our hearts to receive a new level of relationship with Him. Now, we are not only going to church, but we are in training to be used by God. It may still be many months, or even years, before our gift emerges in a mature form; but at least we are en route to our destiny!

At this point, I can hear the response of those young moms with two, three or more little children running around the house: "I want to be more involved at church, but I just don't have the time." So, who said anything about church? More than likely, at this time of your life, *your children* are the gifts God has given you to develop. In time, what you learn while raising your children might be what God will use later. Or, the Lord may have an entirely different task for you once your children mature.

Jesus gives to each of us the tools to do His will. If you have a burden, vision or call from the Lord to some task, the tools will be there to help you accomplish it. You might say, "But, I don't have a college degree." No, but God gave you a brain, and a will, and an anointing to learn what you need to succeed. You say, "But I don't have experience." Maybe not, but you can become a helper to someone who has experience. You can gain the knowledge you need while serving them.

Your gift may be something the Holy Spirit develops and uses where you work. Maybe you just love accounting and working with numbers. Or perhaps you really enjoy cleaning a house from top to bottom (call me if you do!). You might have a great love for cars and the mechanics of motion and repair. *You see, your gift is something you love doing.* It is a *gift* that God gives to you to give to others. More often than not, it is something you enjoy doing. It is a natural extension of your desires and skills.

GOD IS WORKING IN YOU

People often fear that if they truly surrender to the Lord He is going to send them to outer Mongolia or deepest Africa. But, God has been working in you, "to will and to work for His good pleasure" (Phil. 2:13). You see, in God's good pleasure, you will know it when you are doing what He wants you to do. Your gift is not something you're punished with, it is something you can't wait to do.

The main point is that you must use the gifts God has given you. I ask people who complain that they feel worthless, "What are you doing with what God's given you?" If they say, "Nothing," I remind them that Jesus called the slave who did nothing with his resources, "worthless." There may be many reasons we feel worthless, but sometimes we feel worthless because we are doing nothing with our gifts. We feel worthless because, compared to those who are using their gifts, we are worth less.

Now, in God, it is true that our intrinsic worth is not defined by our actions but by the blood of Christ. The fact that Christ died for us tells us, as human beings, God considered us worth sending His Son to die for. We are loved and that alone gives us value. At the same time, while our salvation is secure, our sense of well-being is defined by our *involvement* with the will of God. In other words, our highest calling is what we *are* in Christ. Out of our relationship with Him, what we *do* completes the eternal purpose.

Remember that before Jesus ever did one work of power, He was pleasing to the Father. To truly love God brings satisfaction to His heart. At the Jordan River the Father said about His Son, "This is My beloved Son, in whom I am well-pleased" (Matt. 3:17). Yet, Jesus *completed* the pleasure of God, glorifying the Father, by "having accomplished the work" to which He was called (John 17:4).

Likewise with us, in the first stage of our spiritual lives, finding the will of God is predominantly a learning experience. We repent of sin and turn to the Word. This stage centers greatly upon discovering and applying the basics of the Christian faith and learning what Jesus has accomplished for us at the cross. It is here that we are becoming something in God that He delights in.

The second stage unfolds as we add to our spiritual knowledge the development of our gifts and calling. Now we are

> **Notes**

also being trained in what we are to do. There will be trials and errors as well as false starts and delays. But we are learning and being trained to use our gifts for God's glory, not ours.

The last stage is doing the will of God. Our hearts are poised in worshipful surrender while our hands are busy in purposeful obedience. You see, what we are and what we do are both important to God: in both, we must rise to the character and power of Christ.

It is important to know where you are spiritually. Are you a new believer? Then don't rush ahead in trying to develop a spiritual gift until you are grounded in the Word. Have you been established in the Lord? Then what are your spiritual gifts? I always encourage people to simply examine their hearts and see what their prayer burdens are. Look also at what you love to do. The things we find easiest to pray for are the areas we are often called to serve in.

There are usually several things that you are naturally good at. Because these things are such a part of you, you may not recognize them for what they are: the gifts God has given you. Using these gifts, apply yourself to perform your work in excellence as unto the Lord.

When it's time to bring forth your gift, do so with faith and humility. Believe God for the quickest and deepest work of grace, but be patient if the Lord needs to work wisdom or endurance in you along the way.

If your gift is prophecy or encouragement, develop your gift first in a home group or small prayer meeting among friends. Don't force your gifts on the whole church, but let them grow in these smaller groups. As they mature, the Lord will make a way for you to express His gifts in the larger gatherings.

Remember, according to the parable Jesus taught, if you don't use your gift, you lose it! Use what God has given you for His glory in the earth.

Notes

BOOKS BY FRANCIS FRANGIPANE

CALL FOR QUANTITY DISCOUNTS ON 5+ BOOKS!

This Day We Fight

In this day of advancing evil, will the Church wake up and fight?
Francis Frangipane tells us that the call of God is a call to war. As we stand at the cusp of a major spiritual awakening in our land, the Holy Spirit is ready to impart a fresh anointing to God's people – an anointing that will activate the "war mode" in your heart.
Published by Chosen Books.

A House United

This is a new release of the book *It's Time to End Church Splits*.
Few works of the enemy are as destructive to the Body of Christ as a church split. Once a wedge is driven into the heart of a congregation, the result is usually bitterness, grief, even hatred among those who are called to live together in love. This new edition, has been somewhat revised. A new final section, which includes three chapters, has been added.
Published by Chosen Books.

The Days of His Presence

As the day of the Lord draws near, though darkness covers the earth, the out-raying of Christ's Presence shall arise and appear upon His people! Also an eBook.
Published by Chrisma House.

When the Many are One

Learn how the Christian community - driven by grace, unified in love, and activated by prayer - can bring revival and change to the world. This is a revised and expanded version of *The House of the Lord*. Also an eBook.
Published by Chrisma House.

The Three Battlegrounds

Revised Edition: An in-depth view of three arenas of spiritual warfare: the mind, the church and the heavenly places. Also an eBook.

I Will be Found by You

Perhaps this compilation of teachings from Francis Frangipane will become his most important book yet. It is God's living promise to reveal himself to His people. Also an eBook.

The Power of One Christlike Life

The prayer of a Christlike intercessor is the most powerful force in the universe, delaying God's wrath until He pours out His mercy.

The Shelter of the Most High

Francis gives trustworthy, biblical evidence in the midst of all our uncertainties and fears there is an available shelter from God to shield us. Once you have found this place, nothing you encounter can defeat you. This is a revised and expanded version of *The Stronghold of God*. Also an eBook.
Published by Chrisma House.

Holiness, Truth and the Presence of God

A penetrating study of the human heart and how God prepares it for His glory. Also an eBook.

The Power of Covenant Prayer

Takes the reader to a position of victory over witchcraft and curses. A must for those serious about attaining Christlikeness. Also an eBook.
Published by Chrisma House.

To order, go to **www.arrowbookstore.com**
or call toll free (US only): **877-363-6889**

Discipleship Training Booklets

(5+ AT 40%, 100+ AT 50% DISCOUNT)

COMPILED/FORMATTED FOR GROUP STUDY BY FRANCIS FRANGIPANE

Discerning of Spirits

Chapters: The Gift of Discernment; Eliminating False Discernment; Discerning the Nature of the Enemy; The Stronghold of Christ's Likeness.   #FF1-018M

Deliverance from PMS
by Denise Frangipane

Practical and spiritual helps toward deliverance from PMS.
#DF1-002

Overcoming the Accuser of the Brethren

Chapters: Exposing the Accuser; Casting Down the Accuser; Protected from the Accuser; At the Throne of God. #FF1-017

Overcoming Fear!
by Denise Frangipane

Testimony and keys to releasing the power of faith.   #DF1-003

The Jezebel Spirit

Chapters: Discerning the Spirit of Jezebel; Elijah, Jehu and the War Against Jezebel; Our Experience with Jezebel; Strategy Against the Spirit of Jezebel; Deliverance from the Spirit of Jezebel. #FF1-019

Audio/Video/Download Teachings

PLEASE VISIT WWW.ARROWBOOKSTORE.COM FOR A COMPLETE LISTING.

Jezebel Spirit
#2FF-041 CDs

Your Authority in Christ
#3FF-1264 DVDs

Gift of Discernment
#2FF-1268 CDs $16.00
#3FF-1268 DVDs

Our Shield and Defender
#2FF-1271 CDs $20.00
#3FF-1271 DVDs

Pulling Down Strongholds
#2FF- 040 CDs

Writers Workshop
#2WW-001 CDs

To order, go to **www.arrowbookstore.com**
(see complete resource catalog, current teachings, and conference schedule)
or contact **Arrow Publications, Inc.,** P.O. Box 10102, Cedar Rapids, IA 52410
Phone 1.319.395.7833 or Toll Free 1.877.363.6889   Fax 1.319.395.7353
(VISA/MC/AMERICAN EXPRESS/DISCOVER)
Call for shipping rates and quantity discounts on 10+ books!
Prices subject to change

IN CHRIST'S IMAGE TRAINING MATERIALS

Basic Training Manuals

Study series which pulls together four key areas of this ministry: Christlikeness, Humility, Prayer and Unity. Perfect for leadership teams, prayer groups, Bible studies and individuals who are seeking to possess a more Christlike life. It is strongly recommended that these four manuals be read in sequence, as each study is built upon the truths found in the preceding manuals.

#BT-001   set of 4 - retail $48.00 **Our price $44.00**

IN CHRIST'S IMAGE TRAINING
Online Correspondence Course
available in English and Spanish
Developed by Francis Frangipane

IN CHRIST'S IMAGE TRAINING offers four opportunities for enrollment in Level I training each year: January, April, July and September.

Level I: Certification offers four foundational tracks: Christlikeness, Humility, Prayer and Unity. Completion time is six months.

Level II: Growing in Christ offers further online teaching by Pastor Francis and other national church leaders. Completion time is three months.

Level III: Facilitation provides spiritual equipping for those preparing for ministerial opportunities.

On-site Impartation and Focused Training offers a seminar which can be taken by attendance or via CD/DVD albums. For details watch our website.

Association Graduate students who desire ongoing association with other ICIT graduates, as well as fellowship with other like-minded Christians and churches, are invited to become part of Advancing Church Ministries Association of Churches and Ministries.

In Christ's Image Training center is not a denomination, nor is Advancing Church Ministries (ACM).

Please see our website at www.ICITC.org for enrollment fees and detailed information. 1-319-395-7617, training@inchristsimage.org